GETTING INTO

DIGITAL RECORDING

Digital Audio Basics

Operations

Applications

by Paul D. Lehrman

ISBN 0-7935-5947-2

HAL•LEONARD®
CORPORATION
7777 W. BLUEMOUND RD. P.O. BOX 13819
MILWAUKEE, WISCONSIN 53213

Table of Contents

Chapter 1: Why This Book?

Digital recording has revolutionized the world of audio in the last decade and a half. Just about any recorded music you hear today has existed in a digital format somewhere along the way: if it wasn't recorded on a digital multitrack, then it was mastered on a digital two-track reel-to-reel or DAT. Perhaps it was edited on a hard-disk-based system, or it uses sounds from a digital sampler. If it's on the radio or TV, it may be coming from the digital tracks of a modern video deck, or it's being played from a CD.

Not long ago, the ability to make digital recordings was the exclusive property of big-budget studios and record labels, but a glance at the articles or ads in any recording magazine will tell you that's no longer the case today. Digital two-track masters can be made by anyone with a few hundred bucks for a DAT machine, and those tapes can sound every bit (pardon the pun) as good as masters produced ten years ago on a system costing hundreds of times as much. CD recorders, which produce discs one at a time that can be played on any CD player, are within the reach of many smaller and project-oriented studios.

Most recently, inexpensive multitrack digital recording has revolutionized recording. The cost-effectiveness of recording with the new generation of multitrack digital decks has caused them to invade all levels of the industry — from professional studios where 24-track analog once reigned supreme, to the modest project studio.

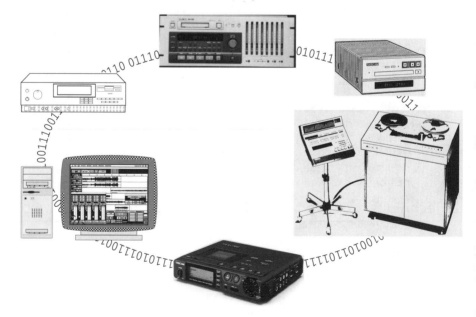

Is Your Future Digital?

So it's easy to feel that, if you're in the business of making recordings, your future is in digital. But is there a way to make the transition from analog to digital painless?

If you've spent any time trying to decide what digital recording equipment to buy, you probably already think the answer to that question is "no way". You've been bombarded by buzzwords, swamped by specifications, and flummoxed by formats. Although you've heard promises that digital will make your back bedroom into a world-class studio and turn you into a world-class recordist overnight, you're not sure. You're worried, with good reason, that you might buy the wrong thing, that it won't do the job you need it to do, or that it will be obsolete before you're done paying for it.

That's why we've put together this book. We want you to make the most well-informed decision you can about the equipment you buy. We'll explain to you how digital recording works, and what much of the jargon that has grown up around it means. We'll tell you which specifications are important, and which ones you can ignore. We'll tell you about the different formats for recording digital audio signals and moving them around a studio. And we'll get into some more advanced topics, like synchronization, for those of you who work with video, film, or multiple audio formats.

What we won't do is lie to you, by pretending that digital will solve all your recording problems. In fact, we'll tell you about some new problems it may create that you may not have thought about. But we'll also tell you how to go about solving some of those problems, so that you end up taking advantage of what digital has to offer, and not get buried by it.

You may even decide after reading this that you'll stick with analog for a while, for all or part of your recording needs. That's okay — a lot of people who make hit records have made that decision too, and digital and analog will continue to co-exist side by side for some years to come. But if you do decide that digital recording equipment is for you, this book can give you the knowledge you need to make informed choices about what to use.

Analog and digital equipment can work side by side

What Digital Audio Can Do for You... and What it Can't

Here's the quick version. The advantages of digital recording can be summed up in two words: fidelity and copyability.

Fidelity means that a good digital system can have ruler-flat frequency response to the limits of human hearing with virtually no distortion, be free of any flutter or wow induced by mechanical problems, and have a dynamic range as large as anything we would ever want in our living rooms or even the quietest studios.

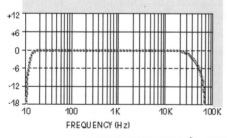

Digital recording can give you flat frequency response and let you make perfect copies

Copyability means that a copy of a digital recording can be a perfect clone: there is no added noise or distortion induced by the limitations of the recording media, and an infinite number of copies of copies can be made with no loss of fidelity.

If that were all that needed to be said about digital recording, this would be a short book indeed, because we could stop right here. Unfortunately, digital recording has its limits, and those limits need to be understood just as clearly, and explored just as thoroughly, as its benefits.

First of all, digital recording imposes certain rules on recording which are much stricter than the "soft" rules of analog recording. Just as digital recording consists of ones and zeroes, there's not a lot of room for fuzziness or error in making digital recordings — it has to be handled correctly or the results will be totally unusable. Secondly, there are quite a few different methods and formats of digital recording, and some are more suited to certain tasks than others. Finally, digital by itself will not make you a great recording engineer. In fact, it may do just the opposite: if your engineering techniques leave something to be desired, it could end up making your mistakes more obvious, and your recordings actually sound worse.

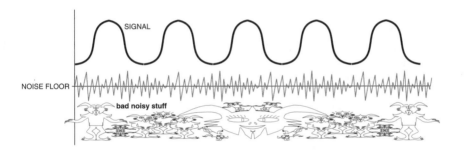

When the noise floor is lowered, the "gremlins"
that were previously underneath it can be heard

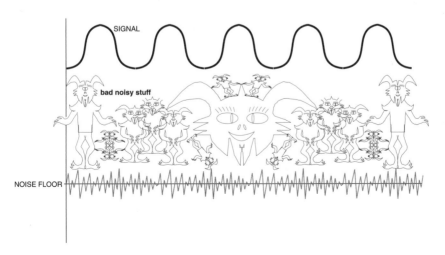

Chapter 2:
What Is Digital Audio?

Before we start talking about equipment, we need to have a basic understanding of what digital audio is all about. This doesn't just have to do with recording: today, digital audio plays a major, even dominant role in signal processing, broadcasting, and communications of all kinds. But the principles are the same, no matter what it's used for.

Sound travels through the air as minute, rapid variations in pressure. The faster the variations, the higher the pitch, and the bigger the variations, the louder the sound. The variations are cyclical in nature, and if you were able to see them as they pass by a single point, they'd look like a continuously changing wave. So we talk about sound being a "waveform".

Digital audio is a method of representing the continuous waveform of sound as a series of discrete numbers. In some ways it's similar in principle to movies or television: in those media, moving images are broken up into individual still pictures, or "frames". When viewed at the proper speed, somewhere from 24 to 30 frames per second depending on the medium, our brains fuse those images into one continuously changing image.

Digital audio also uses "snapshots" of sound, called "samples", to represent the waveform. But it's more complex than film, because of the nature of the way we hear. Sounds are "analog" in nature, continuously varying, with no discrete "jumps" from one pressure level to another, and that's what we expect to hear. Ears can't be fooled the way that eyes can: a sound that "flickers" won't sound right, no matter how fast the flicker is.

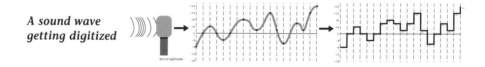

A sound wave getting digitized

This means that digital audio isn't a complete medium for delivering sound information to our ears: it is an "intermediate" medium, and some form of conversion to or from an analog signal must be done at each end of the chain. A microphone creates analog signals, by turning the variations in air pressure into continuously varying electrical signals. In a digital audio system, this "analog" of the real sound gets converted into digital data. At the listening end, the digital data is converted back to an analog voltage, which can then be sent to an ordinary amplifier and speaker, so we can hear it.

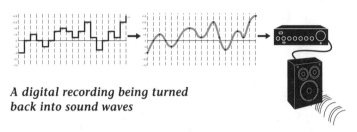

A digital recording being turned back into sound waves

The process of converting analog audio to digital numbers ("A–to–D conversion") involves measuring the instantaneous volume ("amplitude") level of the sound many times each second, and recording that level as a number. This process is called "sampling", and each number that is created in the process is called a "sample", or a "word".

The fidelity of the conversion process is determined by two major factors: the range — the maximum and minimum values — of the numbers available for a given sample; and the speed at which the samples are taken.

The Range of Values: Word Length

How does the range of numbers affect the sound quality? When it comes to representing the volume of a sound, analog audio has infinite resolution — that is, there are an infinite number of values it can take. Whenever you take a sample of the amplitude, therefore, you are actually making an approximation. How close that approximation is depends on the range of numbers you have available to you. If you can use only the numbers 1, 2, 3, and 4, your approximation is most likely going to be very crude. If you can choose from any of 65,536 different numbers, your approximation can be quite good.

The difference between the approximation you make of the value of a signal and the actual value of that signal before you converted it is called "quantization error". We hear it as noise. The greater the range of values you have available for samples, the lower the quantization error, and therefore the less noise the system has — the lower its "noise floor". The difference between the maximum level that can be sampled and the noise produced by quantization error is the signal-to-noise ratio of the analog-to-digital convertor.

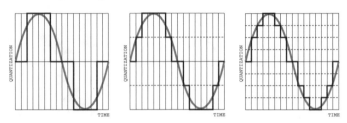

The higher the resolution of quantization, the more accurate each approximation of the signal level is

Digital samples are expressed in binary code — strings of ones and zeroes — because that's the way electronic switches and computers work. (If anyone tells you his digital audio system is better because it works with twos and threes, he's pulling your leg!) Each digit in a binary word is known as a "bit". As it happens, there is a very neat formula that links the number of bits a convertor uses to create a digital sample with the maximum theoretical signal-to-noise ratio of the convertor:

```
S/N ratio in dB = 1.76 + (number of bits x 6.02)
```

This can be (and usually is) approximated into:

```
S/N ratio = 2 + (number of bits x 6)
```

Therefore a convertor that uses digital words that are 8 bits long has a potential signal-to-noise ratio of about 50 dB, which is about what an AM radio is capable of; a 12-bit convertor has a ratio of 74 dB, or about that of a good cassette deck or FM broadcast; and a 16-bit convertor has a ratio of 98 dB, which is about the dynamic range of a symphony orchestra.

These are all theoretical "ideals": in reality, there are other factors, such as the fact that electronic components and circuits don't behave completely perfectly all the time, that tend to lower these numbers slightly.

As far as the number of numbers a convertor can create is concerned, you calculate that by raising 2 to the power of the number of bits in the system: an 8-bit system can have 2^8, or 256 values; a 12-bit system 2^{12}, or 4096; etc.

The industry standard for recording digital audio is 16 bits: that's what CDs, DATs, multitrack digital decks, and digital audio tracks on modern video decks use. We don't really need more than 98 dB of dynamic range in any listening environment, professional or consumer, so this is fine.

However, since "real-world" 16-bit systems rarely achieve the dynamic range they are theoretically capable of, if we really want all of that dynamic range — true 16-bit performance — it can help if we have a couple of extra bits to play with. And even in a digital system, noise is cumulative: if you mix together a lot of digital sources, the noise from each of them will add up, possibly compromising the fidelity of the mix. So the more processing and mixing is done to a digital signal, the more need there is for those extra bits. Therefore many digital applications, like signal processing, all-digital mixing consoles, and even some recording systems, use longer words of 18, 20, 24, or sometimes even 32 bits. Those extra bits help to make sure the final product — which is more than likely going to be a 16-bit recording — is truly as good as a 16-bit digital audio recording can be. Digital delivery systems of the future, like DVD (Digital Versatile Disk), might also use longer word lengths.

Shorter word lengths are acceptable in some situations. Using shorter word lengths means that more sound can be stored within a given amount of memory, and it makes systems easier to design. Many digital samplers — that is, electronic musical instruments which play back sampled sounds in response to keystrokes or MIDI commands — use 12-bit samples and sound perfectly okay, because the dynamic range that is demanded of them is not as large as what is required from a master recording. One early digital recording format, known as "EIAJ" or "PCM-F1", allowed for two different word lengths: 14-bit and 16-bit. The shorter length reduced the dynamic range by 6 dB, but it gave the system two extra bits for detecting and correcting errors (we'll talk about this soon), which made the system more robust, and in some cases actually sound better.

The Speed: Sampling Rate

The other major factor in determining the fidelity of an analog-to-digital convertor is how quickly the samples are taken. If a waveform is to be sampled accurately, there have to be at least *two* samples taken of the waveform, according to a rule known as the Nyquist Theorem. Turn that around, and we see that the sampling rate of a system must be *twice* as high as the highest frequency of the sound that is being sampled. If this rule is not observed, "foldover" or "aliasing" occurs, which consists of unwanted frequencies showing up in the digital signal.

Here's an illustration of how aliasing occurs. If we take a convertor with a sampling rate of 20 kHz, and feed it an analog signal at 15 kHz, the samples that are taken don't represent different parts of a single cycle, they represent different parts of *different* cycles. The convertor doesn't know this, however, and assumes the samples are from within a single cycle. The frequency of the signal the convertor *thinks* it's looking at happens to be equal to the difference between the input signal and half of the sampling frequency, or 5 kHz, and this 5 kHz "alias" is dutifully passed through the recording chain and eventually to our ears. Obviously, this situation is something to avoid.

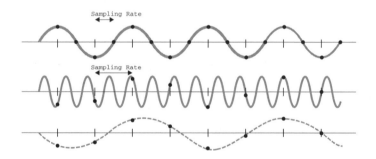

Trying to sample a sound higher than half of the sampling rate produces errors, because the convertor cannot get two samples of each cycle. This is called "aliasing".

The frequency response of the human ear, at its best, extends to about 20 kHz. Therefore, to cover the entire range of possible frequencies, sampling rates in digital convertors must be at least 40 kHz. It is entirely possible, however, that sounds above 20 kHz may be generated in a recording situation (just because we can't hear them doesn't mean they're not there), and so to prevent those unheard sounds from causing aliasing, they need to be filtered out. This could be done with a "brick-wall" low-pass filter, which simply eliminates all frequencies above 20 kHz.

On a practical level, however, such a filter is impossible to build, and even if it were practical, it would probably introduce some kind of distortion (most likely phase-related) in frequencies below 20 kHz, particularly if it was an analog circuit. To get around this, sampling rates are usually higher than 40 kHz, and filters that don't have to work quite so hard — their frequency response slopes down above 20 kHz, instead of trying to abruptly cut everything off — are employed to prevent aliasing.

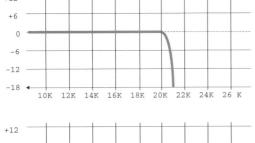

The higher the sampling frequency is above the audible range, the gentler the anti-aliasing filter's slope can be

The most popular sampling rates for digital recording are 44.1 kHz and 48 kHz. CDs are recorded at 44.1 kHz. Much professional audio production is done at 48 kHz. You may come across lower sampling rates in certain applications. As with shorter word lengths, lower sample rates mean less room is needed for storing signals, and circuits are easier to design. Some signal processors, like digital reverbs, use a lower sampling rate on the principle that very high audio frequencies don't reverberate much in nature, so they can be ignored by the processor.

Lower sample rates, such as 22 kHz and even 11 kHz, are common in multimedia, where the need for quality sound often takes a back seat to fancy visuals, and storage space is at a premium. You can also find slower sampling rates used in some broadcasting applications, like Direct Broadcast Satellite, which is in use in Asia and Europe, and carries 32-kHz digital audio. Although it's not used very much, the Digital Audio Tape (DAT) specification allows for 32-kHz sampling (as well as 12-bit operation) either to double the capacity of a tape, or to allow recording of four channels of audio. Finally, you may encounter odd sampling rates like 44.056 kHz. These are used when digital audio is being synchronized with video, which we'll talk about later in the book.

Converting It Back

The reverse process — creating analog signals out of digital ones so that we can hear them — is called, not surprisingly, "D-to-A conversion". The numbers are fed into a device which generates a voltage whose level corresponds to the value of the sample. This results in a waveform that looks like a staircase. This waveform is smoothed by a low-pass filter (analog or digital) which takes out all the high harmonics above 20 kHz, and turns the steps into straight lines or smooth curves. This signal is now a nearly perfect reproduction of the original input signal, and it can be sent to an amplifer and speakers, and then to your ears.

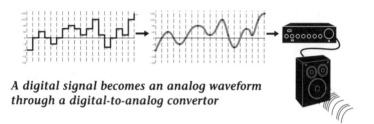

A digital signal becomes an analog waveform through a digital-to-analog convertor

Buffering

Another thing you should know about while we're still talking theory is buffering. On an analog tape recording, the speed that the tape moves at controls the speed — and pitch — that the sound plays at. Minute speed changes caused by mechanical imperfections in the transport, or by stretching of the tape, result in small changes in pitch, which we hear as wow and flutter.

Digital audio recording does things differently. Digital audio signals must have a master clock controlling their speed, so that the beginning of each sample word occurs at exactly the right time. If it doesn't, bits will get scrambled, producing unpredictable — but predictably nasty — results. This master clock runs at a speed equal to the sampling rate (or some multiple of it), and is generated by an ultra-stable crystal.

But a mechanical transport, like a cassette or reel-to-reel tape deck, cannot be counted on to run at an absolutely steady speed all the time. To compensate for this, digital data coming off of the tape is put into a "buffer" or storage area before it is converted to analog. The buffer may have more or less data coming into it, depending on whether the tape is fast or slow, but its output will always be at exactly the right rate, because it is controlled by the sampling-rate crystal.

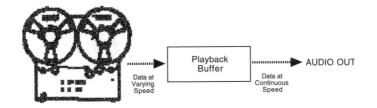

Buffering makes sure that the data is always converted at the correct rate, even if the tape speed varies

Think of a pail of water with a hose coming into it, and a precisely-designed valve at the bottom to let the water out. The amount of water the hose delivers may go up and down, but the valve makes sure that the water leaves the pail at a constant rate. That's how digital audio buffering works. It means that digital recording systems do not suffer from any speed variations, and why in spec sheets under "Wow and flutter" it usually says "unmeasurable".

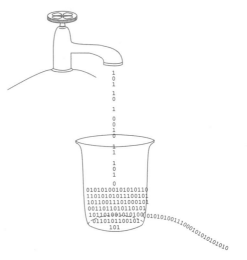

It is important that the sampling-rate "clock" be very steady. Any variations, no matter how small, in the clock can result in what's called "jitter", which can have subtle but audible effects on the sound. Noise, distortion, high-frequency phase problems, and degraded stereo separation can all result from poor jitter control. High-end digital systems often go to great lengths, using all sorts of electro-mechanical feedback loops, to minimize jitter.

Chapter 3: The Two Basic Rules of Digital Recording

So now we see that digital audio offers us linear frequency response, a wide dynamic range, and freedom from speed problems. But while digital makes some things easier, it also imposes its own restrictions. Making numbers out of analog signals and storing them on tape (or something else) is a very different process from recording analog signals. We'll get into more details about what this means in practical terms a little later, but for now, understand and keep in mind the following rules of digital recording:

• Rule 1: The limit on the loudest signal you can record is absolute.

If you push an A-to-D convertor with a signal louder than it can accept, it will literally chop off the peaks of the waveform, and the result will be distortion of a particularly ugly sort. This is very different from analog recording, which gradually increases distortion as levels increase, and the distortion is not always unpleasant — many engineers think it adds "warmth" or "fatness" to the sound, and often use it deliberately.

A signal too loud for an analog-to-digital converter to handle causes hard clipping

• Rule 2: The limit on the *softest* signal you can record is also absolute.

Analog tape has an inherent noise floor, which is the hiss level of the tape, but you can hear signals that are actually softer than the noise. Listen to a long fade-out on a master tape: the signal keeps going for a while even after you can hear the tape hiss clearly. But the bottom of a digital dynamic range is not "transparent": if the signal level is below the quantization level for the least significant bit, you won't hear it, period.

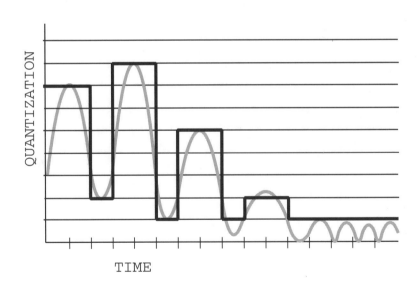

*If the signal level is lower than the lowest
quantization level, it won't be converted*

Chapter 4: Making It Better

Although digital audio can sound very good, in practice it is not perfect. Designers and engineers are constantly striving to make systems work better, and new solutions are constantly popping up. Some of these solutions turn out not to be as successful as their designers had hoped, or end up being more trouble than they are worth, and so they fade away after a brief period in the limelight. Many innovations, however, have turned out to be significant, and have become important features of digital audio systems.

Dither

We said just a moment ago that digital signals cannot go below a certain level, or they will disappear. Actually, the situation is worse than that. As the level of a signal goes down, the quantization error, which at higher signal levels is heard as noise, becomes distortion. That's because the fewer number of bits available to describe the waveform will turn a nice, smooth wave into something that looks like a staircase, or at the very bottom of the dynamic range, a square wave. So the signal doesn't fade gracefully into hiss — it becomes buzzy and distorted, before it disappears into complete silence.

To combat this, A-to-D (and sometimes D-to-A) convertors usually include a circuit called a "dither generator". Dither is noise, similar to analog tape hiss, which is added to the signal at a very low level, usually one-third to one-half of the lowest quantization level. Its purpose is to keep low-level signals from being overly quantized. With a constant source of noise present, the lowest quantization level is simply never reached, and the signal, instead of being distorted, lies on top of the noise. Adding noise to a signal sounds much more natural to us than hearing it distorted into square waves, and so although dither slightly *decreases* the overall signal-to-noise ratio of a digital system, the net effect is that it makes low-level signals sound *better* than they would without it.

Adding dither helps low-level signals

Oversampling

Oversampling is a technique that reduces the load on the filters in a convertor. It works by putting extra samples into the bit stream and raising the sampling rate to accomodate them. The effect of this is to change the frequency of any aliasing products so that they are far above the audible range. This means that the filter used to remove those aliasing products can have a very gentle action, much more so than a filter which has to work close to the top of the audio range. The gentler the action of the filter, the fewer problems it potentially will create on sounds within the audible range.

When the signal is reconstructed in 16-bit format at its normal sampling rate, the extra samples are removed, in a process called "decimation". Oversampling is a very popular technique in both professional and consumer digital audio equipment, because it makes filter design much simpler. Systems can be found which work at anywhere from two to 64 times the original sampling rate.

Error Correction and Compensation

Error correction is an important aspect of digital audio recording, and good error correction is essential for a system to work properly.

In any recorded medium, errors are inevitable. When a piece of analog tape has a mechanical defect, there's a dropout. This can be a barely-noticeable momentary dip in signal level or change in timbre, or it can be a complete loss of signal. Analog dropouts are caused by defective media, such as particles of oxide flaking off of a tape, or by dirt finding its way between the tape and the head.

Digital media are subject to the same mechanical problems as analog media, and dropouts can occur there to. However, because the data density of a digital recording is much higher than that of analog, the results of an error are invariably much more obtrusive: at best, the signal disappears and reappears with a click, and at worst the missing data can produce horrible grungy noises. For this reason, almost all digital audio recording systems use some form of error correction to make sure errors don't happen.

Error correction schemes all use some kind of data redundancy: if a bit or a "burst" of bits is lost, the system can look somewhere else for the missing data. The most foolproof way to use redundancy is simply to record everything two or three times, and in fact "double recording" is used in some systems. However, this uses up a lot of extra storage space, and so it's not always practical. Instead, various schemes using what's known as "parity checks" are used.

In a simple parity system, each 16-bit digital word is sent along with one extra bit, known as the parity bit. If the number of 1s in the word is even, the parity bit is "1". If the number of 1s is odd, the parity bit is "0". When the data is read, if the bit count of the word and the parity bit don't agree, the system knows that there has been an error, and it ignores the data.

data	parity bit	OK?
1001011000110010	0	OK
0001111001110010	1	OK
1101101011011010	0	error!
0001111010101010	1	OK
1010101001110011	1	error!
1110011010101010	0	OK
0010011011011001	0	error!

A simple parity-check system

A parity system this simple is not sufficiently sophisticated for digital audio, but more elaborate systems based on the same principle are. Among these are "Cyclic Redundancy Check Coding", or CRCC, systems, which use complex mathematical processes to create parity words out of blocks of data. CRCC can detect both small, random errors and large bursts of erroneous data. There are a number of different CRCC systems, and you will encounter these with names like "Reed-Solomon codes", "Hamming codes", or "convolutional codes".

Once the system has detected an error, its next job is to reconstruct the bad data. If the error is brief, the system can simply look at the data surrounding it, and guess at what the missing word is supposed to be by repeating the previous sample, or by interpolating a new value that is between the previous sample and the next one. In practice, digital audio systems look at multiple samples simultaneously, and can fix errors of several thousand or even tens of thousands of bits in real time, without any audible artifacts.

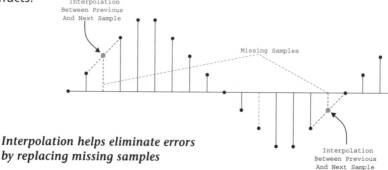

Interpolation helps eliminate errors by replacing missing samples

20

Another technique that can help minimize errors is to avoid recording the data linearly on the medium, and instead break up each word and shuffle the bits around so they appear in different places. This technique is called "interleaving", and its advantage is that if a microscopic error occurs, it won't obliterate whole words, but just parts of several words. With sufficient redundancy, there's a good chance that what remains can be used to reconstruct the original data.

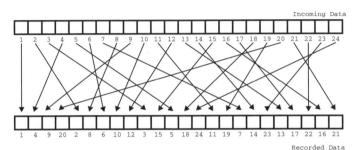

Interleaving breaks up the digital data into different places so that if there is a physical problem with the medium, the data can be more easily reconstructed

In the worst case, when so much data is erroneous or missing that the system cannot reconstruct the missing samples, it will simply mute the output, on the principle that no sound at all is better than the sound of digital distortion. Even this radical step does not necessarily harm the sound: mutes that last for less than a few milliseconds are usually not audible.

Error correction is at the heart of digital audio's copyability. There will always be errors introduced in recording and playing data to a mechanical medium, but with powerful error correction, the effect of those errors can be minimized and even completely eliminated. That's why, in a well-designed and maintained system, the 200th generation of a digital recording sounds identical to the first.

Chapter 5:
PCM, AES/EBU, S/PDIF, etc.

Okay, we've digitized our signal, filtered out the aliases, and checked it for errors. Now what? Well, we need to get it onto some form of recordable medium. To do that, we first have to send it down a wire. That means transmitting the data as some kind of signal.

We can send the ones and zeroes all by themselves, but that can lead to interference and reliability problems. For example, if several 1s are sent back to back, the receiver may not be able to distinguish between them, and may miscount the number of bits, or even read them as a single, albeit rather long, "1". It's better to encode, or modulate the data onto another kind of signal, which also contains timing information so that the bits are always counted correctly. There are many methods by which digital data can be modulated onto a signal, and different ones are used in different applications. When it comes to digital audio recording, however, by far the most popular is known as Pulse Code Modulation, or "PCM".

Pulse Code Modulation uses a steady pulse wave which runs at the sampling frequency (or a multiple) of the A-to-D convertor. While the amplitude of each pulse is the same, the starting time and width of the pulse vary according to the value of the sample being encoded. For example, if a 4-bit word 0001 were being transmitted, the pulse would turn on only during the last quarter of its cycle. If the word 1110 were being transmitted, it would be on for the first three-quarters of its cycle, and off for the last quarter.

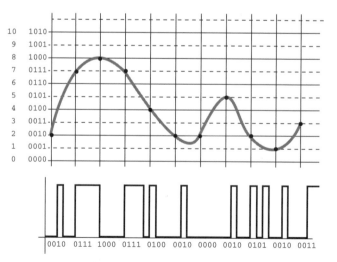

Pulse Code Modulation (PCM) changes the starting time and width of a pulse according to its digital value, but the amplitude is always the same

Pulse Code Modulation can be used with any word size, and digital words can be broken up into smaller segments if desired. By using a higher frequency, two channels of audio can be multiplexed onto a single PCM signal, with numbers for left and right channels alternating. This, in fact, is the most common way of encoding, transmitting, and storing stereo digital audio.

Other coding methods

You won't come across them too often, but it's worth noting that there are other types of digital encoding besides PCM (which is sometimes called "linear PCM" to differentiate it from the others) that are used in some circumstances. There's "Floating Point PCM", in which the digital word is divided into two parts, with an imaginary decimal point in the middle. The digits before the decimal are called the "exponent" or "gain select", and they determine a range of values within which the digits *after* the decimal point operate. Using this scheme, a 13-bit word, for example, can cover a dynamic range equivalent to a conventional PCM scheme with 17 bits. The drawback is that because the number of digits after the decimal point keeps changing, the quantization noise goes up and down with the level, and for many types of program material, this is unacceptable.

Other coding schemes include "Companding", in which the signal is compressed as it is digitized and expanded as it is converted back to analog; "Differential Encoding", also sometimes called "predictive encoding", in which instead of storing the entire digital word for each sample, only the difference between successive samples, a much smaller word, is stored; and "Delta modulation", which is a very fast form of differential encoding in which only a single bit is sampled. Various modifications and even combinations of these techniques can be found in specialized applications.

A sophisticated alternative system called Adaptive Transform Acoustic Coding is used in the MiniDisc system. It incorporates principles of "psychoacoustic masking", which state (to simplify greatly) that because sounds in some frequency and volume ranges will cover up other sounds, you don't really need to record those other sounds. MiniDisc systems, which are both recordable and erasable, can store digital data in about one-fifth the space required by a linear PCM system.

Although it is not used much in music recording studios, the fidelity of a MiniDisc system can be excellent. Many radio stations use them to play spots and short programs , broadcasters and filmmakers use them to record sound in the field, and they can also be found in self-contained multitrack mixer/recorders, replacing the traditional analog cassette tape.

Transmission

The next question is, what kind of signal does the digital data get Pulse-Code Modulated onto? Here we have a number of choices, and these fall into the family of digital audio transmission or "interfacing" formats. All of the formats in common use today can handle sample rates of 32 kHz, 44.1 kHz, or 48 kHz.

Sony formats

Many early digital recording systems used PCM techniques to put the digital audio signal onto a video signal, which could be recorded on a conventional video deck. The two channels of a stereo signal were multiplexed together onto a single video line. Sony developed two different formats: a professional version, known as "SDIF", for "Sony Digital Interface Format" (and now known as "SDIF-1", to differentiate it from its successor, SDIF-2); and a consumer version, known by its various model names, which included PCM-F1, PCM-501, and others. Due to its high fidelity and low cost, the consumer version actually ended up being very popular among professionals, particularly classical music recordists, who used inexpensive consumer-format videotapes — VHS and Beta — for recordings. The professional version, which was found in the model PCM-1600 and PCM-1610 convertors, was for several years the preferred system for mastering CDs, generally using 3/4" U-matic professional-format videotape for the recordings.

Today, Sony CD mastering systems are based on the PCM-1630 convertor, which uses the SDIF-2 protocol. (The convertor can also read SDIF-1 signals, so that older tapes can still be used.) SDIF-2 allows up to 20 bits of audio data, along with various control and synchronization bits in the same digital word. Each cable in an SDIF-2 system handles only a single audio channel, and so two cables are necessary for stereo. In fact, when copying audio from one SDIF-2 system to another, a third cable is needed to handle "word clock", which is a special signal that ensures the two channels remain in perfect synchronization.

AES/EBU

The AES/EBU formats have become the most popular method of transmitting digital audio between devices. Created by a joint effort of the Audio Engineeing Society (AES) and the European Broadcasting Union (EBU), there are actually two versions of the format, which are very similar but not quite identical.

The AES/EBU protocol is very comprehensive. It puts both audio channels on one cable, and has timing information built in: the speed of the signal is dependent on the sampling rate. This is called "self-clocking". It is designed to be sent over fairly long distances (at least 100 meters) using ordinary twisted-pair cable. It uses a method of bi-phase frequency modulation (not unlike SMPTE time code, if you happen to be familiar with the way that works) which makes it "polarity independent" — you can't hook up an AES/EBU cable out of phase, and it doesn't matter which pin is "hot".

The AES/EBU digital word is 32 bits long. In the professional format, 24 of those bits can be used for audio data (for one channel). The other bits provide information from the transmitter to the receiver like time of day, sampling frequency, address of the data to make sure synchronization is being maintained, synchronization words, and various other data. Because so much data is on the line, the effective frequency of an AES/EBU signal is 64 times the audio sampling rate, which works out to 3.072 MHz at 48 kHz sampling rate.

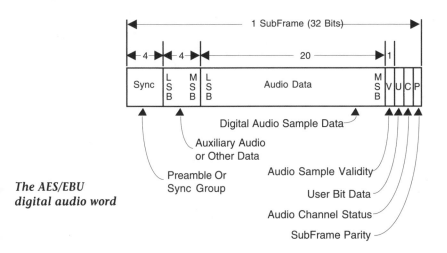

The AES/EBU digital audio word

The professional format uses a balanced line, terminating in XLR connectors, with pin 1 as the ground and the signal on pins 2 and 3. The voltage of the signal should be between 3 and 10 volts. The professional format is sometimes known as "AES3".

The consumer format differs in a few ways. Only 20 bits are available for audio, and the cable used to connect units is either unbalanced coaxial, terminating in RCA (phono) plugs, or is made from optical fibre. The signal level is quite a bit lower, around 0.5 volts. Some of the non-audio data bits are defined differently from the professional format.

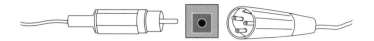

Connectors for AES/EBU signals:
RCA plug and fiber-optic socket (for consumer format),
and XLR plug (for professional format)

Despite these differences, it is sometimes possible to connect professional and consumer units directly to each other. For example, if a digital recorder with professional inputs has particularly sensitive and forgiving input circuitry, it may be able to accept a signal from a digital sampler, DAT deck, or CD player that has consumer outputs.

There's a lot of confusion about the names of these formats. When a manufacturer refers to its unit's "AES/EBU" connectors, it generally (but not always) means they are of the Professional variety. Consumer-format connectors are commonly called "S/PDIF", which stands for "Sony/Philips Digital Interface Format", but in fact S/PDIF and AES/EBU consumer are not *quite* the same. They are completely compatible, but certain non-audio bits are defined differently in the two formats. Just to make things more murky, the two AES/EBU formats are sometimes referred to as "IEC-958 Type I" or "CP-340 Type I" (professional) and "IEC-958 Type II" or "CP-340 Type II" (consumer).

MADI

MADI, for "Multi-channel Audio Digital Interface" (and certainly not to be confused with "MIDI") can be thought of as the multitrack version of the AES/EBU standard. It uses a single video-quality coaxial cable terminated with BNC plugs, or an optical fiber cable, to carry up to 56 channels of audio. The samples can be up to 24 bits long. The data format is identical to that of AES/EBU, except for the first four bits (and it obviously runs much faster). This makes "breaking out" a MADI line into individual AES/EBU signals quite simple from a programming standpoint.

MADI can support sampling rates higher than 48 kHz, by doubling up channels, so that the space that normally is used for two data channels is used for one. The specification also allows for a separate line to accompany a MADI cable to carry synchronization information, which can be useful in many circumstances. MADI is also sometimes known as "AES10".

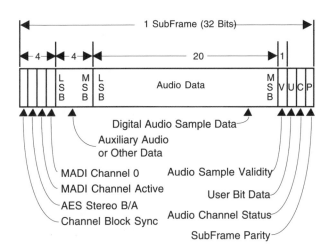

The MADI digital audio word

Proprietary Formats

A number of manufacturers have come up with unique interfacing schemes. Most of these, after failing to gain support from other manufacturers, have disappeared. One example was the ProDigi format used by multitrack recorders made by Mitsubishi and Otari, which was similar to SDIF-1, but not compatible with it.

Yamaha used a proprietary interface for its digital 8-track recorders and mixers, which is still available as an option for its current line of digital mixers. It uses a 25-pin connector carrying a cable pair for each pair of audio channels, plus a separate pair for word clock.

The formats that promise a longer life are those of the modular digital multitrack recorders. For Alesis-compatible machines, there is an optical interface that carries eight channels of audio on a single cable, and can handle sample lengths up to 24 bits. For DA-88-compatible decks, TASCAM developed an interface, called "TDIF-1", which uses a 25-pin connector to handle the eight channels of audio.

Format Conversion

The biggest problem confronting users of devices with different formats is converting signals from one format to another. While an S/PDIF output can sometimes be connected to an AES/EBU professional input, and while MADI and AES/EBU formats are easily converted back and forth, other formats can present serious problems when you try to put them together.

For example, if you wanted to mix a digital sampler with an S/PDIF output, with audio from a D2 video deck in AES/EBU Professional format, through a Yamaha digital mixer, and have it feed an ADAT deck, you are talking about at least three format convertors (S/PDIF-to-Yamaha, AES/EBU-to-Yamaha, Yamaha-to-Alesis), even if all of the devices are running at the same sampling rate — which they very well may not be. Format convertors can be very expensive, and so most studios try to avoid using mixed formats, but with the growth of modular digital multitrack decks, more companies are building format convertors, and prices are finally coming down.

Even if all of your digital signals are in AES/EBU format (either professional or consumer), you will have problems mixing them in the digital domain. For example, let's say you have a digital sampler, a DAT, a hard-disk audio system with AES/EBU outputs, and a D2 video deck . Since the format requires no separate word clock cable, most AES/EBU devices cannot slave to an external clock. Therefore, if you want to mix all of these sources as digital signals, you first have to pass them all through a sample-rate convertor, which will synchronize them all to a single clock source, and then they can goto a digital mixer.

For those stuck in digital format hell, however, there is often a very simple answer: go analog. Rather than spend thousands of dollars for custom convertors to keep data in the digital domain, you may very well be better off simply converting the incompatible signals to analog, and mixing or processing them that way, then convert them back again to digital for the final product.

Professional equipment — and these days, a lot of consumer gear as well — can usually be counted on to have very high quality digital-to-analog conversion circuitry, and so going through a couple of conversion stages for the purpose of mixing or processing shouldn't harm the signal much, if at all. Note that we're not talking about *recording* in analog — that's a very different matter, and generation noise when going through several recording stages is a serious issue.

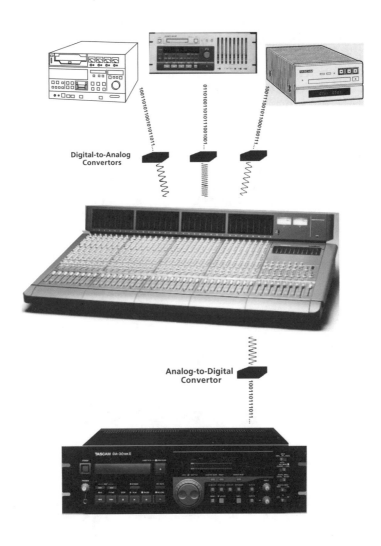

Mixing different digital sources is sometimes a lot easier in the analog domain

Chapter 6: Disk Systems

So we've got our analog signal converted to digital, the digits are coded, and modulated onto a signal and sent down a cable. The next step is to record this information onto something.

As we said earlier, the first digital audio recordings were made on videotape, and many systems still use videotape as the recording medium. Videotape is relatively inexpensive, is easy to come by, and has the wide bandwidth needed to record multiple channels of digital audio. But other, specialized tape formats for recording digital audio have come into being as well. In addition, a new kind of recording medium has appeared in recent years that offers an entirely new approach to recording and editing, and that is the computer disk.

Computer hard disks (also known as "Winchester" disks) make a very useful medium for digital audio because of one particular attribute: they allow "random access" to the data — that is, any data anywhere on a disk can be played at any time. Audio information can be stored in any order, in long, contiguous segments or in short, disjunct ones. Long segments can be broken up into shorter ones, known as "regions", which can be individually manipulated.

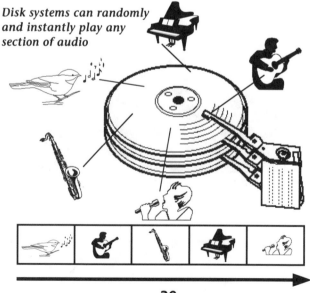

Disk systems can randomly and instantly play any section of audio

This "non-linear" characteristic of disk systems makes them particularly useful for editing. Imagine you have an hour's worth of audio on a reel of tape. You want to make a new track using, in order, 15 seconds of sound at the beginning of the original tape, 30 seconds just before the end, 45 seconds at about 20 minutes into the tape, and 60 seconds at the 10-minute mark.

There's no way you can tell any tape recorder to play this back in a single pass — you either have to physically splice the various sections of the tape together, or electronically edit it by making dubs of the different sections and putting them together in the exact order you want.

A disk-based audio system, however, can be told to jump to different spots on the disk and play those pieces of audio one right after the other. The spots can be as far apart as you want, and you can designate as many of them as you want — the system should be able to play them in the sequence you specify without missing a single sample.

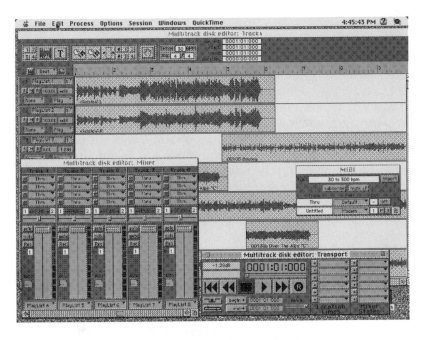

Disk editing software lets you freely
arrange different sections and tracks

Earlier we talked about buffers as a way to eliminate speed-variation problems from digital audio. Disk-based audio systems need buffers for another reason. Even though jumping from one spot on a disk to another can happen very quickly, it is not instantaneous. It takes a certain minimum amount of time, known as the "access time" (sometimes called the "seek time"), to do this. The access time of a disk system can be anywhere from 5 to 100 milliseconds, depending on the type of disk. In order for the audio to continue to play uninterrupted, a buffer, big enough to hold sufficient audio data to cover the longest possible jump, is needed. So if the maximum access time is 100 milliseconds, and you are using a sampling rate of 48 kHz, the buffer must be able to handle 4800 samples for each channel of audio.

There are other important advantages to using disks for audio recording. One is that because you are manipulating jumping instructions — known as "pointers" — instead of the actual audio data, you can record an essentially unlimited number of "tracks" of audio.

You don't have to erase one track in order to record another in its place, so you can keep every take in a session. When you're done recording, if you like the first four bars of the second take of a sax solo, and the next two bars of take 12, and the last 8 bars of take 4, you can "splice" them together merely by telling the system to point to each of those pieces of audio in turn. Plus, you can quickly try out different arrangements and versions of the edits, and any edits you do can easily be "undone", because there's no actual alteration of the audio data. This kind of editing is known as "non-destructive" editing, because the original audio recording stays intact.

You can also slide tracks in time, by tiny or large amounts, without re-recording them. You can repeat sections of audio without using up additional storage space. Many systems allow you to put a crossfade between one segment and the next, with variable length up to several seconds, to make the transitions smooth. Some of these systems use computer RAM to store the crossfades, while others create new pieces of audio on the disk which contain nothing but the crossfades.

Although disk-based systems can be used as conventional-style recorders, they are at their best in situations where the emphasis is on manipulating sound — such as editing — rather than on recording it. They're very popular for producing dance mixes, and also in editing and post-production of soundtracks for film and video, where many elements from a large number of different sources — music, sound effects, ambience, and dialogue — need to be cut and pasted, mixed, and placed precisely in time. The amount of flexibility that disk-based audio offers the composer, music editor, or sound editor could not be conceived of just a few years ago, and remains truly unsurpassed.

Disk-based systems are available both in two-track and multitrack configurations. Two-track systems are used for editing, mastering, and simple recording jobs, such as voiceovers and small classical or jazz ensembles. Multitrack systems range in size from "Portastudio®"-like four- and six-track, self-contained units, to professional 24-track systems with multiple disks and interfaces. With multitrack systems, you can have the equivalent of a 24-track tape deck on your computer screen, with instant access to any piece of any track, anywhere on the tape. The best systems offer automation, digital equalization, reverb and other effects, synchronization to SMPTE time code and/or digital word clock (see Chapter 9), and even the ability to play (and follow) a video right on the computer screen.

If the disk system runs on a computer which can also be used for MIDI sequencing, the computer can present you with an interface in which audio tracks and MIDI tracks are shown simultaneously, and can be moved around and edited relative to each other. Audio tracks can be automated in terms of volume and stereo pan position just like MIDI tracks, and in some cases processing operations like pitch or length changing can be applied to audio segments just as if they were MIDI notes. This way of working — using the disk for vocals and other non-MIDI-able sounds, while taking advantage of MIDI's compactness and flexibility for rhythm tracks and other instrumental sounds — is a wonderful way to make a small studio sound like a much bigger one.

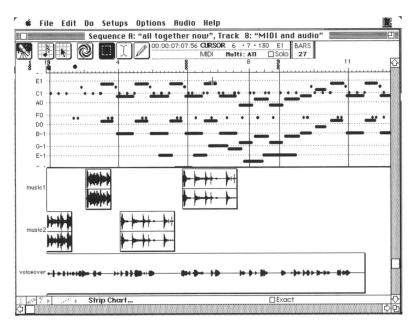

Some systems let you mix audio and MIDI tracks

Types of Disk Systems

Disk-based audio systems come in two flavors: dedicated systems in which all of the components are made by one manufacturer, or systems that run on popular personal computers such as the Apple Macintosh, or IBM PC. In the latter case, usually only the software and the audio input/output and processing hardware is supplied by the system manufacturer, while storage is handled by devices made by the computer manufacturer or third parties. The nice things about a computer-based system are that you have the computer available for other tasks, and you can easily add more storage relatively inexpensively, by buying devices appropriate for that computer — usually in the form of SCSI (for "Small Computer Systems Interface") drives.

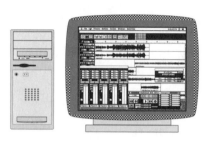
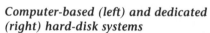

Computer-based (left) and dedicated (right) hard-disk systems

However, adding storage sometimes presents problems. Audio puts very heavy demands on disk drives, and a drive that might be just fine for word processing or graphics on a particular computer may be too slow for audio. When pushed to its limits, it may lose data, corrupt files, or even self-destruct. Therefore, you must be very careful when buying third-party disk drives for a computer-based audio system: they must meet the requirements of the audio manufacturer in terms of access time, as well as the speed at which they can pass data, known as the "throughput".

Dedicated systems, because the manufacturer has complete control over which components are used in the system, can be more robust than computer-based ones, and can use proprietary hardware to achieve greater speeds. However, it is usually more costly to upgrade them, because you can't use off-the-shelf components, and repairing them is also more of an issue, because you can't just grab a hard disk from another computer to replace a disk that fails.

Dedicated hard-disk audio systems, by the way, are very often referred to as "workstations", although that word has now been used for so many different types of products, it's difficult to give it a precise definition.

There are also systems that have characteristics of both types: they use high-speed data protocols, such as SCSI2, for improved performance, and the manufacturers provide storage devices along with their audio hardware, but they still use a personal computer for the user interface and for file management. Higher-speed data exchange means that more simultaneous tracks of audio can be recorded or played on one disk: depending on the cleverness of the software and the speed of the hardware, digital systems can get anywhere from 2 to 24 tracks off of a single hard disk.

A special category of hard-disk audio system uses magneto-optical disks as the recording medium. A handful of manufacturers, including Akai and Fairlight, make these systems. They have an advantage in that the recording medium is removable and relatively inexpensive, but because the disk itself is quite a bit slower, the editing flexibility of these systems is not as good as on Winchester-based systems. In addition, disks from different manufacturers' systems are frequently not interchangeable.

While systems that run on computers usually require external hardware, in the form of a circuit card or a standalone box connected to the computer, some computers, such as Power Macintoshes (based on the PowerPC chip), can handle 16-bit audio directly, and require no extra hardware to record and play back analog audio.

Because of the way computers are designed, however, it is difficult to keep extraneous noise out of the audio signal, and cost considerations mean that the D-to-A and A-to-D convertors are not of the highest quality. Therefore the performance of such systems, while it can certainly be very good, is typically not as good as systems that use external hardware.

Drawbacks to Disk Systems

The chief problem with disk systems is their limited storage capacity. It takes approximately 5 megabytes of disk space to store one minute of a single track of digital audio, and if you're doing an entire CD or film score with lots of tracks, you'll find space gets used up quickly. Once you finish a project, you have to erase all of your tracks from the disk and start over before you can go onto the next one, unless you have huge amounts of storage available.

This is a particular problem with systems that use fixed, internal hard drives. Systems that are expandable, using multiple SCSI devices, can do better, but even they will fill up eventually, since you can't keep adding drives indefinitely.

Some disk systems get around this by using removable media, so you can take the audio files off the system and store them just like tapes. The media tend to be expensive: Syquest removable cartridges, for example, come in several formats, from 44 megabytes (about 9 track-minutes) to 270 megabytes (about 54 track-minutes) and cost from about $30 to $100. This situation promises to improve thanks to a recently-developed technology called the "Jaz" drive, which gets 1000 megabytes (1 gigabyte, or 400 track-minutes) on a cartridge that costs around $100. This puts storage cost in the same ballpark as professional analog tape formats, but it's still far more expensive than the new multitrack digital tape formats, as we will see.

A cheaper alternative is a backup system, in which all of your tracks are stored "off-line". One such system is computer Digital Audio Tape, known as "SCSI DAT", because it connects to a SCSI port just like a hard drive. SCSI DAT tapes are quite similar to, but not really interchangeable with audio DAT. The recording medium is very inexpensive — less than $20 for a tape that can hold 2000 megabytes — but the backup process is very slow: that tape takes 90 minutes to fill, during which time the computer can't be doing anything else. And the re-load process is just as slow: you have to allow 90 minutes to get the data back onto your disks before you can run a session. There are also other types of tape backup systems, made by companies such as Exabyte and TEAC. In fact, owners of digital multitrack decks such as Alesis' ADAT and TASCAM's DA-88, are finding that these make attractive general-purpose backup systems as well, thans to the low price of their media.

Another type of backup is removable magneto-optical (M/O) cartridges, which come in several formats, holding from 128 to 1300 megabytes, and ranging in price from about $40 to $100 per cartridge. These also need dedicated backup time, but are quite a bit faster than tape. They also use the SCSI protocol. New formats are constantly being developed, with larger storage, faster access, and lower prices.

Perhaps the coolest backup technology is recordable CDs and CD-ROMs, which produce audio or data CDs one at a time in real time, or faster. Just a couple of years ago these were affordable only by the largest of production houses, but prices on the recorders themselves are now around the $1000 mark, putting them with reach of many musicians and project studios. The blank CDs, which can hold up to 650 megabytes of data, can be found for less than $10. Besides backing up data, recordable CDs can be used to make test pressings, or to send a client home with something to listen to that's better than analog cassette.

Like vinyl record cutting lathes of old (and unlike the MiniDisc systems mentioned in Chapter 5), recordable CDs cannot be erased and re-used—although erasable CDs are in development. Many recorders demand that you record the entire CD in one continuous pass (those that let you start and stop are called "multi-session" recorders). However, these incoveniences are far outweighed by the fact that you can play a CD you've recorded on any standard player.

Which brings up another issue, which is interchangeability. Unlike tape, in which most manufacturers follow industry standards, so that a recording made on one machine can easily be played back on another, digital audio files recorded with one system often will not translate to another. Even if both systems use the same kind of hardware, for example a Macintosh computer and a common digital audio interface, the files will not be compatible. Or the audio files themselves will play on the two systems, but the edit data, which includes editing points, crossfades, automation, or effects, will not translate. An effort is being made to overcome this with the "Open Media Format", or "OMF". Systems made by companies that subscribe to this format can export their editing information, as well as the audio data itself, to other OMF-compatible systems.

Finally, there is the question of file integrity. Because you are dealing with what are essentially computer files, rather than the stream of audio data that you would find on a tape, there are more things that can go wrong. If a file "header" contains a serious error, or if the disk's directory somehow gets damaged, the system may lose the file and never again be able to open it — even though there's nothing wrong with the audio data! Some systems which use multiple disks to store large files will effectively lose the entire file if any one of the disks is damaged. These concerns make backing up even more crucial.

Chapter 7:
Tape Systems — 2-track

As revolutionary as disk-based digital audio has been, it has not, and will not, replace tape as the medium of choice for many applications. Most audio as it is delivered to the end user, whether it's a radio broadcast, a CD, an analog cassette, or a score for a film or video, is linear, and so a linear storage medium still makes perfect sense. Even audio for a random-access application, like a computer game, needs to be delivered to the developer in linear chunks.

Tape is cheap, readily available, easily interchangable among machines that use a common format (even removable disks sometimes have trouble if they are transported from one system to another, theoretically identical, system), and provides its own "backup" — when you're done with it, take it out of the machine and store it on the shelf.

Of course, editing with tape is not nearly as flexible as editing from a disk, and most digital audio tapes cannot be physically spliced the way analog tapes can (although two formats, as we shall see, do allow this), but electronically editing digital tape to combine different takes or tracks into a single recording is a straightforward process that can also be extremely accurate. This editing is usually done entirely in the digital domain, so many generations of edits can be made without compromising the sound quality at all.

This chapter will talk about two-track digital tape formats; we'll discuss multitrack formats in the next chapter.

Many of the first digital audio tape formats, as we said earlier, used videotape cassettes for storage. Videotape makes an excellent medium for storing digital audio because of its high bandwidth: a stereo digital audio signal requires a bandwidth of at least 44,100 bytes x 16 bits per byte x 2 channels per second = about 1.4 MHz. A typical video system provides over 2 MHz of bandwidth. The PCM data is frequency-modulated onto the various subcarriers within the video signal, and is recorded just the way an ordinary video signal would be. Instead of being "pixels" that make up a video picture, each dot in the video frame represents a digital audio bit. In general practice, Sony PCM-1600 through 1630 convertors were used with 3/4" U–Matic videotape, and PCM-F1 convertors were used with 1/2-inch consumer-format decks, Beta and VHS.

Videotape allows such a high bandwidth because the mechanism that reads the tape is spinning, or "rotary", unlike an analog audio deck, in which the head is stationary. A video head assembly consists of two, and sometimes four heads, mounted on a cylindrical drum that spins. Therefore, the movement of the tape against the heads is a lot faster than if they were standing still.

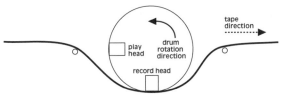

A spinning head assembly allows the tape to behave as if it's travelling much faster, and record a wide bandwidth

The path that the heads takes over the tape is called a "helical scan": it is a series of closely-spaced diagonally-oriented tracks. There are also sometimes straight ("longitudinal") tracks at the edges of the tape, which are used for control information to make sure the spinning heads and the tape are in perfect sync; for analog audio; and in some formats for SMPTE timecode.

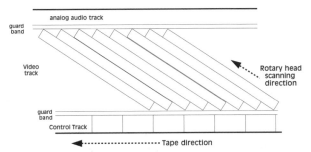

Vdeo tracks are recorded at an angle on the tape, while control tracks and analog audio are recorded longitudinally

Modern videotape formats, all of which still use rotary heads, incorporate digital audio along with (as opposed to in place of) the video signals: D-1, D-2, D-3, and D-5 formats (there is no D-4) can record four tracks of 44.1- or 48-kHz PCM audio, using 16-bit or larger words. 8mm video decks can record two tracks of 10-bit nonlinear digital audio (which actually gets compressed to 8-bit) , at a sampling rate of 31.5 (in the US and Japan) or 31.25 (in Europe) kHz.

DAT ("R-DAT")

The rotary head concept was adapted into what is now the most common industry format for two-track digital audio: "R-DAT", for Rotary (head) Digital Audio Tape, or simply "DAT". DAT machines are similar in principle to video machines, but are optimized for audio. A lot of the extraneous information needed to handle video signals is eliminated. The amount of tape in contact with the head at any one time (the "head wrap") is smaller, which means both heads and tape last longer, and the tape tension is lower, which also improves head life.

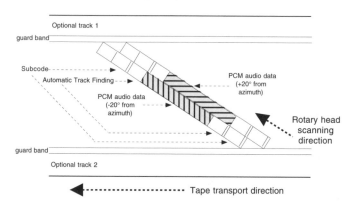

DAT tape records alternate tracks at different angles, and encodes subcode and track finding information with the audio

The two heads on the drum are tilted in opposite directions — one is tilted so its azimuth is +20° from vertical and the other is -20° — so that the information each prints to the tape is oriented differently. This cuts down on crosstalk between adjacent scans, which means that information can be packed very tightly onto the tape. There are no longitudinal tracks: the control tracks (known as ATF, for "automatic track finding") that keep the heads and tape in sync are built into the helical tracks. The format is set up, however, so that indexing and other information can be read while the tape is in fast-forward or rewind, allowing very rapid access to individual segments or cues on a tape.

TASCAM DA-30MKII DAT deck

DAT tapes can be recorded and played back at sampling rates of 32 kHz, 44.1 kHz, 48 kHz. Many "consumer" decks do not allow digital recording at 44.1 kHz, so that ordinary folks cannot digitally duplicate the CDs they buy. However, this precaution, which was included in the initial DAT spec adopted in 1986, was not enough, as far as the American record industry was concerned. They delayed the introduction of DAT into the consumer market until they had additional protections, and it is this reason why DAT never took off as a consumer medium (although it is highly successful with pros).

The record industry's first protection attempt was an audio-modifying scheme called Copycode, which fortunately was abandoned when it proved destructive to the quality of the signal. It was followed, more successfully, by a purely digital scheme called the Serial Copy Management System, or "SCMS".

SCMS, which was adopted into US law through the Home Recording Rights Act in the waning days of the Bush administration, puts an inaudible digital code into every digital recording. This code tells a device receiving it whether the program material can be legally copied as many times as the receiver wants, only one time, or not at all. Commercial CDs, for example, can be copied once in the digital domain, but then that copy cannot be copied further.

Unfortunately, recordings from an *analog* source, such as a recording studio with an analog mixer, when they are put onto DAT, are also encoded with a SCMS signal that says they can only be copied once. This makes it a bit difficult for the recordist to make usable safety copies of his or her own digital masters. Fortunately, "professional" DAT decks are not required to include SCMS circuitry, and so these — although they are not necessarily much more expensive than "consumer" decks — are much more useful in the studio, whether it's a home-based project facility or a downtown multiroom complex. Some consumer or "semi-pro" decks have and internal switch or jumper that can be changed to defeat the SCMS system, and there are also outboard devices available from some manufacturers that can remove the SCMS "flag" from a recording.

Although DAT is strictly a two-track format, there is a way to get it to read and write SMPTE time code. It involves reading and writing information to the subcodes in the signal. Although DAT subcodes don't actually lend themselves well to dealing with SMPTE (the two frame rates do not factor easily into each other), a DAT machine with SMPTE does all the necessary fancy arithmetic quite invisibly, and to the user it simply appears as though the deck has a third track for the time code. Time code DAT machines usually have four heads instead of two, and tend to be quite expensive.

Stationary Head Designs

There is another way to do two-track digital audio recording, which uses not spinning heads, but fixed ones. To achieve the necessary data density for digital audio with a stationary head, the audio is often recorded on multiple parallel data tracks. Most stationary head formats use tape on open reels, just like analog.

Stationary-head digital recorders often have more heads than you'd expect. This is because, unlike analog recording, getting a single head to do both recording and playback is very difficult, and so when you are overdubing or punching in a track, there will be a time disparity between what you are recording and what you are monitoring off the tape — just like an analog deck that has three heads but no "sync" mode. To overcome this, a second record head, used only for sync recording, is placed after the playback head, at the same distance that separates the main record head and the playback head, so the delays cancel each other out.

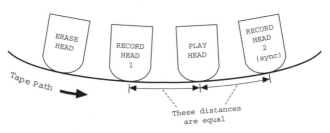

A second record head allows overdubbing and punching without delay problems

One popular stationary-head format (actually, it's a family of formats) is "DASH", for Digital Audio Stationary Head. When used for two-track recording, a DASH tape puts 8 data tracks and 4 auxilliary tracks on 1/4" tape, and runs it at 7.5 or 15 ips (assuming 48 kHz sampling — 44.1 kHz is also available, and uses a slightly slower speed).

The digital audio data is split up so that the samples are "sequenced" along the tracks: the first sample for the left channel goes to track 1, the second sample to track 2, the third, to track 3, and the fourth to track 4, and then the sequence starts over. The right-channel audio samples do the same thing on tracks 5 through 8. One of the auxilliary tracks is used for control and synchronization information, to mark the start of each data block. The others are used to record ordinary analog versions of the signals being recorded digitally, so you can cue the tape just the way you can an analog tape; and/or for time code.

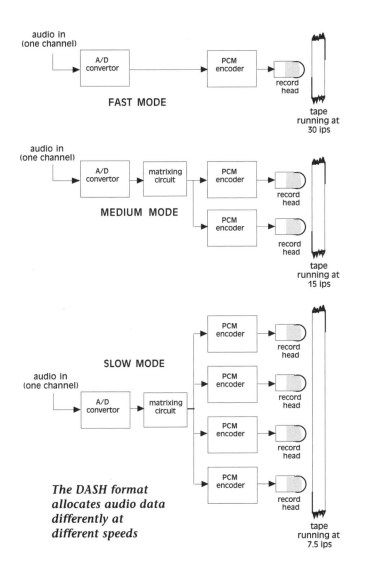

The DASH format
allocates audio data
differently at
different speeds

One of the advantages of DASH tapes is that you can physically splice them: DASH machines have such sophisticated error correction that if they encounter the gross error caused by a splice, they will automatically create a smooth crossfade over the splice point, which in most cases will be inaudible.

Another advantage of the DASH format is that by increasing the tape width and/or the speed, you don't improve fidelity (as you do with analog tape) but you can record more tracks: in fact, up to 48 channels of audio can be recorded on a 1/2" DASH tape running at 30 ips. More about this in the next chapter.

One type of DASH recording is called "Twin DASH". In this format, which is used only for two-track recording, all of the data is recorded on two sets of tracks simultaneously, and the order in which the data is divided up is reversed on the second set of tracks: one set of tracks will alternate odd- and even-numbered samples, while the other will go even/odd. This makes the recording much more robust and resistant to errors, but it also means that twice as much tape is used per audio channel.

There is also an "S-DAT" (Stationary Digital Audio Tape) format that was adopted at the same time as R-DAT, but no commercial S-DAT machines have ever been produced.

Chapter 8:
Multitrack Tape Systems

The development of multitrack digital audio recorders has progressed in a different way from two-track: the first successful ones were stationary-head machines, while rotary-head multitrack machines — similarly based on videotape technology — are a more recent development.

DASH was the first accepted industry standard for "professional" multitrack digital audio, and Sony, Studer, and TEAC/TASCAM all make DASH machines which are completely compatible with each other. As we saw in the previous chapter, DASH tapes can be 1/4" or 1/2"; can run at 7.5, 15, or 30 ips; and can record at 44.1 kHz or 48 kHz sampling rates. The wider the tape and the faster the speed, the more tracks you can record. In addition, there are two levels of data density on DASH recordings: Normal and Double. The maximum number of tracks you can record on normal-density tapes is 24 , while on double-density tapes you can record up to 48. Machines with Double-density heads can read Normal density tapes without trouble; machines with Normal-density heads can read Double-density tapes, but they will ignore every other track.

TASCAM DA-800/24 DASH deck

Rotary head digital multitrack

Stationary-head multitrack digital decks are very expensive, and have been beyond the means of all but the highest-end studios. Rotary-head decks have changed that. One of the reasons that they can be made inexpensively is that many of them take advantage of advances made in consumer video technology.

The first rotary-head multitrack deck was Akai's A-DAM, which put 12 tracks of audio on a standard 8mm video cassette, running at slightly more than four times its normal speed, allowing 21-1/2 minutes of audio on a 90-minute cassette. This format has not been adopted by other manufacturers, and although it is far less expensive than most stationary-head multitracks, it is still not cheap.

Like rotary head two-track machines (and unlike stationary-head decks, analog or digital), the *entire* audio signal — all 12 tracks — is always recorded at the same time. When you punch in or overdub a track, instead of recording just that one track, all of the tracks are lifted from the tape and put in a RAM buffer where they are digitally combined with the new track, and then the new composite signal is recorded back to the tape in place of the old signal. This works okay, unless someone trips over the power cord while you're doing an overdub, in which case all of the tracks will be lost.

The two formats that are doing the most to bring digital multitrack capabilities to the smaller studio are based around S-VHS and Hi8mm video technology. S-VHS-based machines are available from Alesis, Fostex, and Panasonic; Hi-8mm machines are available from TASCAM and Sony. The prices on these machines are comparable to, or even lower than the prices small studios are used to paying for analog multitrack decks, while the sound quality is equal to the mega-buck digital decks of the recent past.

S-VHS (left) and Hi-8mm (below) tape cassettes

Although both formats can only handle eight tracks of audio, multiple machines can easily be linked together — up to 16 at once, for 128 tracks — with sample accuracy, using a dedicated word clock line. Remote controllers are available that treat multiple machines as if they were a single deck, so the user doesn't have to worry about synchronization, offsets, pre-rolls, and other issues that traditionally are part of multiple-machine systems.

A helical scan recorder cannot put separately addressable "tracks" on a tape, the way that a stationary-head deck can, so when the audio is recorded, the eight tracks are recorded in discrete "packets" of data. When a track is overdubbed or punched, the record head switches on and off very quickly to make sure only the data packets that the user wants to change are affected.

These two formats are known collectively as "modular digital multitrack." There are differences between them, and although these differences may seem a little esoteric to the digital recording novice, they will become more significant as the medium develops and becomes more popular.

The S-VHS format (known as "ADAT") uses a standard VHS video transport, specially modified to run at three times normal speed. The high speed is necessary because of the nature of the control track used: as in a conventional video recording, the control track is linear, not helical, and is written and read by a stationary head. The digital audio is recorded by rotary heads in a helical scan pattern, and the control track records one pulse at the beginning of each helical scan. In order for that pulse to be sample-accurate, the tape has to run at a relatively high speed.

This affects the amount of time you can record on a tape: a standard 120-minute tape will only record 40 minutes of audio. It also makes fast-forward and rewind times longer. There are two ways to fast wind a VHS tape: with the tape wrapped around the head assembly, which allows monitoring of the signal on the tape, and unwrapped, which doesn't. Winding with the tape wrapped is certainly the more useful mode, but the system is not designed to do this all the time — if you shuttle back and forth too much with the tape wrapped, you risk wearing out both the tape and the heads. Furthermore, it's slow — winding with the tape unwrapped is twice as fast.

Longevity and stability are issues in other areas as well. Linear tracks, even in the best video systems, are more affected by tape stretching, head wear, and mechanical aging than helical tracks, and once a control track is damaged, the tape becomes forever unplayable.

VHS transport and tape technology have been around since the mid-'70s, and compared to more recent developments in tape technology, VHS tapes have a low data density and are potentially more volatile, so that data may potentially not be as safe.

Hi-8mm is a newer format: the first Hi-8 video decks appeared in the late '80s. Like DAT, all Hi-8 decks — video and audio — put the control track into the helical scan, using Automatic Track Finding. The rotating head drum has four heads, so the control track is read four times as often as if it were being read by a stationary head. This means that in multitrack digital audio applications, the tape can run at very nearly the same speed it does for video: 108 minutes of audio can be recorded on a 120-minute video tape.

The tape path in a Hi-8 system is much simpler, with fewer loops and turns than a VHS transport, which allows faster winding of the tape. The system is also designed so that in fast wind, the tape is always in contact with the head drum, which means that you can monitor it at fast speed without worrying about excess wear. The result is that shuttling a Hi-8 tape while monitoring it is up to 7-1/2 times faster than the same operation on an S-VHS audio deck, and even in the smallest studio, time is money — particularly when doing mixdown or post-production.

And speaking of money, because Hi-8 tapes run on audio machines at nearly the same speed as they do with video, the cost of tape works out to be more than 60% lower for Hi-8 than for S-VHS. The smaller tapes also mean that less storage space is needed, which is another consideration for high-traffic studios.

The magnetic coating on Hi-8 tape is made from metal particles, and it has a much higher density than earlier video formats, which is why so much data can be put on such a small tape. It also has higher coercivity (meaning it takes more energy to record onto) and higher retentivity (meaning it's harder to erase), with the result that long-term data storage on a Hi-8 tape is more secure. The tape shells themselves add to that security: a Hi-8 tape, when it is not actually in the deck, is always fully sealed, so the tape is never exposed to air or dust. Compare that with VHS, in which a length of tape is always hanging outside the shell — flip a VHS cassette over and you'll see.

TASCAM DA-88 digital multitrack recorder

An interesting use of Hi-8mm digital decks is in mastering applications for 24-bit stereo audio. 24-bit sampling is popular in some high-end audio applications, and there is no way for standard two-track decks to handle it. But hardware is available that splits the 24-bit signal into two parts, and records each part on one track of an 8-track deck, thus using four tracks for a stereo signal. This gives you a super-high-fidelity system at a very low price, both for the hardware and the recording media. You can also, of course, use all eight tracks to record four tracks of 24-bit audio.

Chapter 9: Synchronization

And now a word about synchronization. The word is: **Caution!**

Synchronizing digital audio recordings to each other and to the outside world is a very complex subject. We'll touch on a few basics here, but if you want to know more about it, we'll refer you to the sources listed at the end of this book.

There are a number of different types of situations in which digital audio sources need to be synchronized to something. Here's the simplest: you are copying a stereo digital recording from one device to another. In order for the copy to be correct, the transmitter and receiver have to have their sample-rate clocks running at exactly the same speed. How this is done depends on the transmission format. In SDIF-2, MADI, and some proprietary formats, a separate cable carrying word clock makes sure that the two are in sync. Word clock is simply a very accurate digital timing pulse that tells the receiver how fast the digital data is being transmitted, and exactly where each data word begins.

In AES/EBU (and S/PDIF), however, there is no separate word clock line, because the format is "self-clocking". Therefore the receiver gets its timing information from the audio signal itself, and locks its sample-rate clock to the incoming signal.

Synchronizing two digital sources

Now let's look at how to synchronize two digital audio *transmitters* to each other, as when we are mixing diverse sources — say two multitrack decks, or a multitrack deck and a hard-disk audio system — in a mixing session. Let's think about how we would do this in analog: we would stripe SMPTE time code on a track on each deck, designate one as the master and all of the others as slaves, and use a transport synchronizer to control the speed of the slaves so that their time code follows perfectly the time code on the master.

With digital audio, there is an additional problem: signals that are locked together must be synchronized at the *sample* level — every bit in every data stream must occur at exactly the same time as the corresponding bits in all of the other data streams. If this doesn't happen, there will be periodic clicks in the sound, as the sample clocks "walk away" from each other and create conflicting data. Even if two sources' clocks are accurate to within one part in 100,000,000, there will be a click about every minute.

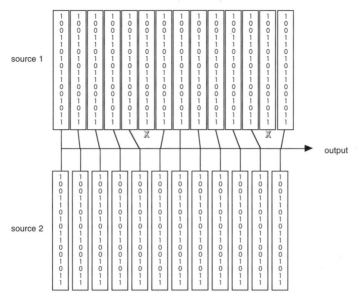

If data streams aren't perfectly in sync,
audible errors result from missed samples

SMPTE time code isn't good enough to handle this. It only guarantees accuracy to within about 4 microseconds. Digital audio clocks must be accurate to (at 48 kHz) 0.6 microsecond, and only word clock can provide this. With SDIF-2 and the other transmission formats that have separate word clock cables, there is no problem with multi-machine systems — designate one as a master and the other as slaves, and you're in business.

But AES/EBU doesn't have a way to separate word clock from the audio. So, as we discussed earlier, if you have two or more different sources of AES/EBU digital audio that you want to use together, either they need to be equipped so that they can respond to an externally-generated sample-rate clock, or they need to go through a sample rate convertor. Some manufacturers of high-end AES/EBU digital audio systems have taken the former approach and put in provisions for sending and receiving word clock over cables separate from the audio. Unfortunately, since this is not codified in the AES/EBU standard, there is no single way to do this, and so different manufacturers use different methods, many of which are incompatible with each other.

Synchronizing to video

Working with digital audio in a video environment opens up a whole 'nother can of worms. Again, looking at an analog system will help us understand the issues.

In a conventional SMPTE-based system, like one in which an analog audio deck is locked to a video deck, the information sent from the master to the slave is in two parts: "Where are we?" (the time code frame number, or location) and "How fast are we going?" (the time code speed, or frame rate). Transport synchronizers for analog decks handle both types of information to ensure smooth and accurate operation: they first locate themselves to the proper frame number, using a function called Frame Lock, and then closely follow the speed of the time code, using a function called Resolve.

Some disk-based digital audio systems, on the other hand, respond to only one or the other, and this can create problems. If a system responds only to frame *numbers*, by starting to play when a particular frame appears and then running on its own internal clock (a practice known as "Edge Triggering"), it's possible that over time the audio and video will drift away from each other, and the sound of a person's voice may no longer match his lip movements. On the other hand, if a system responds only to the frame *rate*, then it has no way of knowing when it's supposed to start playing what, and its location has to be set by hand every time it plays. This is, needless to say, a rather inefficient way to run a studio. So in any kind of professional audio-for-video application, a digital audio system must be able to handle both Frame Lock and Resolve.

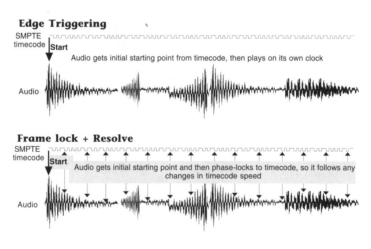

When audio is triggered without being resolved to the video, it may drift. With Phase Lock, it remains in sync.

In most post-production facilities, all of the video and audio equipment is locked to a very stable and accurate synchronization signal known as "house sync". This signal, which runs at the frame rate of video, is used as a timing source for SMPTE time code generators, to make sure they're all running at the same speed. It can also be used to generate word clock for synchronizing digital audio systems. Rather than have a separate convertor connected to each digital audio system, there should ideally be only one word clock generator in a studio, to prevent any discrepancies that may arise between different convertors. Therefore, facilities that use a lot of digital audio not only have house sync running through cables in the walls, they now often have word clock as well.

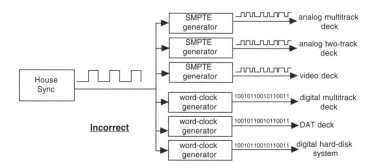

Just as a video studio has only one source of house sync, a digital studio should have only one source of word clock

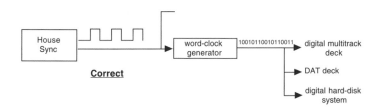

And one more thing. Although SMPTE time code counts 30 frames of video in a second, in the real world (at least, in the NTSC television standard used in North America and Japan) there are actually only 29.97 frames in a second. This has been a factor in digital audio recording since the beginning: because early digital recorders were based on video formats, and because 44.1 kHz and 48 kHz don't divide very well by 29.97 (although they both divide very nicely by 30), many of those systems actually used a slightly different sampling rate: 44.056 kHz or 47.952 kHz, which are known as "Pull Down".

This solved the problem of how to get the digital audio data to fit into a video frame. But another problem remains: how to get a non-video-based digital audio source, like a DAT or multitrack deck, which runs at exactly 44.1 kHz or 48 kHz, to lock to video running at 29.97 frames per second (fps).

One solution is to have the digital audio deck lock to the video (both the sample-rate clock and the transport speed), in which case it will run slightly slow — 0.1%, to be precise. However, if the audio was recorded at one sample rate and played back at another, it won't match the picture. Therefore, when you are doing audio for video, it's important to make sure that you are always — during recording, editing, and playback — locked to a source of video sync. Some systems will not let you do this, however, and you will find, sooner or later, that they are unsuitable for video post-production work.

In the case of one video system, the digital format known as D2, the digital audio tracks are set up to run at exactly 48 kHz, so there is no synchronization problem when recording audio on that format. Other problems crop up when transfers are made between video and film, since film runs at exactly 24 fps, which converts easily to 30 fps but not to 29.97. When adjustments are made in the video speed to make the transfer, the audio has to be adjusted as well.

Modern systems, including modular digital multitracks, can sync to either 29.97- or 30-frame SMPTE time code without any hassles or special tricks. Most decks let you select the time code frame rate when you put a new tape through an initial "formatting" procedure. In most cases, you should select 29.97, even if you have no plans to lock the tape to video. You don't lose anything by making that choice, and you could avoid a lot of confusion further down the road.

As the field of digital recording evolves, other solutions for syncing multiple sources, both audio and video, will emerge. Keep your eyes and ears open, and when looking at new technologies, always think to yourself whether they meet all the criteria for what you are going to need.

Chapter 10: Techniques for Digital Recording

We've already gone over the golden rules of digital audio: never exceed the highest level possible in an A-to-D convertor, and never go below the lowest quantization level. But there are many other, more subtle rules and techniques that need to be paid attention to when you bring a digital tape deck into your studio.

Digital recording will solve only one set of problems: it removes from the recording chain the limitations imposed by analog tape. But when you do that, you might find you have a whole new set of problems to deal with, problems elsewhere in the recording chain that the noise, distortion, or wow and flutter of analog tape were covering up.

Digital recording, contrary to what some people think, will not make everything you do sound great. Sometimes, in fact, it will do just the opposite. With its low noise and wide frequency range, digital recording is very unforgiving of mediocre equipment or poor recording techniques. If you've been making sloppy recordings with analog tape, making them digitally will actually cause them to sound worse, because any garbage on the tape will be much more obvious. So you've got to pay attention to what you're doing like never before. If you want to take advantage of what digital recording has to offer, you're going to have to spill some sweat over the details.

The Recording Environment

Let's start with the room you record in. Low-frequency noise from air conditioners, fans, or traffic rumbling by won't be masked by tape noise any longer. If the building creaks or you've got mice running through the walls, you'll now hear them clear as day on the track. If the room has odd reflections or resonances, they'll show up too. You may find that you need to mic vocals and instruments much closer than before, to keep room noises and effects to a minimum. You also may want to get some acoustic treatment for the walls and ceiling, like tiles or blankets, to make the room more neutral sounding. If the extraneous noise level is really high, you may find you have to build an isolation booth, with insulated or even double-studded walls, ceiling, and floor.

Noises that you couldn't hear before will be very obvious on digital tape

...Myowww...

Now your mixing room. If it's noisy, chances are you've been putting stuff on the tape that you've never heard. But when the tape is digital, and your client takes it into another studio which is quieter (or even into his living room, if he lives in a quiet neighborhood), he's going to hear all that stuff. So you might have to bite the bullet and do some major acoustic treatment on your control room. Short of that, you may be able to get away with investing in a really good pair of headphones — ones that go around the ear, and shut out the room noise — and use them regularly to make sure your mixes are really quiet.

Mics and Mixers

Next, there's microphones. Unbalanced, high-impedance mics might be okay for a bar gig, but the hum, buzz, radio-station interference and other electronic flotsam and jetsam they like to pick up will be painfully obvious on a digital track. Good-quality balanced mic lines are essential, and so are pop filters for vocalists and wind filters for horn players (especially now that you're close-micing more). Your mic collection itself might need upgrading: that falling top end that works so well to keep feedback down in a club will make your vocals sound dull against the instrumental tracks you're recording, which now sound crisper than ever. Learn about which mics work well with what kinds of voices and instruments, and select intelligently.

It's a frightening prospect, but the mixing console you use for tracking or mixdown may not be up to the task of dealing with digital tracks. What's quiet, clean, and flat enough for multitrack analog cassette may sound noisy, dirty, and shrill under the clear, unforgiving light of digital.

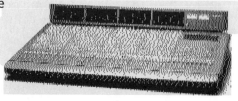

The worst culprits are often mic preamps: inexpensive consoles use simple circuits and cheap components to bring the feeble currents produced by microphones up to operating level, and they may cause the sound to become noisy, distorted, or colored. If this is happening to you, you may want to invest in some good-quality outboard mic preamps. Another common culprit is EQ: poorly-designed equalizer circuitry can add distortion, phase shift, and "ringing" to a signal. If your onboard EQs are causing audible damage, get some outboard EQs and patch them in when you need them.

Even if your board is good enough, you may not be using it to its best advantage, and that will become obvious when you record digitally. Every console has a way to set up the input trims, faders, subgroups, and masters so that each stage of amplifcation — each "gain stage" — is operating at its optimum level: not too hot so it distorts, and not so quiet that noise becomes a factor. If you've never studied your console's gain staging, and never learned how the manufacturer says it should be set up for best performance, now's the time. Read the manual, or call the dealer or manufacturer, and ask about gain staging. You may be surprised at the answers.

Power amplifiers also have an optimum operating range — cranking the volume controls on the things up full is not always the way to go — so check out your monitor amp's operating manual to make sure you're getting the most out of it, too.

You may have to change your mixing technique with digital tape, especially when it comes to dealing with empty tracks. Whereas before, the amount of noise that an open fader on a blank tape track or a silent synth added to a mix was unimportant, now when you mix to a digital master, the source noise, or even the console's inherent noise, may be apparent. Therefore, you're going to have to get used to muting unused tracks to make sure the mix is as clean as possible. Make sure the mute switches on your console are quiet: if they cause clicks, they're worse than useless. Many reasonably-priced consoles now have MIDI-automatable mutes, and if you're using a sequencer anyway, these are easy to work with and can be a big help.

Other Concerns

Those old "walkperson" headphones that you and the musicians in your studio have been using to listen to cue mixes aren't going to cut it any more. The lower noise floor of digital recording will allow headphone leakage to shine through on every track, which you certainly don't want. You should use phones that leak as little as possible: maybe the same ones you're using to check mix noise, or maybe less expensive ones, but definitely ones that seal around the ears.

If you use a lot of synthesizers and other unbalanced equipment, you no doubt already have some experience fighting ground loops. Digital, not surprisingly, makes grounding problems worse by making them more obvious. Your old tape recorder may have had its own noise problems around 60 Hz, and so those ground loops didn't seem so bad, but rest assured your new digital one won't. Learn about good grounding practices, and try to tie all your equipment to a common, well-designed ground. Even balanced lines can have ground loops, or be susceptible to radio interference (not just from broadcast stations, but also from nearby CBs, taxicabs, cellular phones, and — yes! — computers), so if you find you're hearing junk you hadn't noticed before, it might be wise to replace that old war-surplus wiring with new high-quality cable.

Be careful with processing and effects. Cheap reverbs and delays can introduce distortion, or sound harsh and "granular", especially in the reverb tails, which you may have gotten away with before, but you won't any longer.

Using compressors and limiters correctly is critical. Perhaps in the past you've just twiddled the knobs until they sounded good, without really knowing what you were doing, but now you're going to have to learn what's really going on. If you use them wrong, you'll hear "noise pumping" or the signal will sound unnaturally squashed, and there will be no tape noise or tape-induced compression to cover it up.

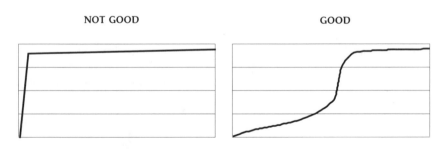

NOT GOOD

GOOD

This compression curve will make a
noisy signal even more noisy

This compression curve will even out the
dynamics without increasing the noise

Speaking of which, the relatively warm distortion and compression effects that you often get when you push the levels on analog tape are something that *won't* be available to you any more. Lots of people like, and even rely on those effects, but digital tape won't produce them — you feed it an overloaded signal and it just sounds horrible. So to get that effect, you'll have to use real compressors and learn how to make them do that. If you want smooth distortion, guitar-amp simulators or tube preamps or processors are the way to go.

And while we're on the subject of levels, just where is "0" on a digital tape? Well, 0 is actually the *top* of the dynamic range, which is a level you *never* want to hit. Some people, therefore, calibrate the 0 VU point of their analog console to the -12 dB point on their digital recorder, which gives them 12 dB of headroom to play with. Others use the -15 dB or -16dB point, for even more headroom. Headroom is important, but you also don't want to throw away too much of the dynamic range just to make sure you're not overloading the analog-to-digital convertors.

Some level meters will suggest where "0" is

So keeping levels steady on a digital recording is just as important, and maybe even more so, than on analog. It's sort of like playing "The Price Is Right": you want to get the levels up as close to 0 as possible, without ever going over. Keeping your signals clean and your levels steady involves staying on top of everything we've mentioned up to this point, especially watching your source levels and gain staging carefully. Take extra advantage of compressors and limiters, and what they can do to help.

Getting it Out the Door

Finally, what about when the tape leaves your studio? When you deliver a digital tape to a high-end professional studio, a post-production facility, or a pressing or duplication house, what information do you need to give them? Do you need to put tones on the tape the way you do with analog?

Well, since there are so many different formats and sub-formats of digital recording, some information is essential: what kind of machine you recorded the tape on, the sampling rate, the number of selections, and the timings, both overall and for each selection or cue.

Be sure when you're assembling your final master that each selection is indexed correctly: some decks will increase the index number every time you hit the Record button, even if you're erasing a previous take, and the result will be missing index numbers which will cause the people who are playing your tape to scratch their heads in confusion over what you wanted.

You also have to make those folks aware if you are using pre-emphasis. Pre-emphasis is a leftover from the early days of digital and there really isn't much justification any more for using it, but some decks give you that option anyway, and if you take it, you've got to tell the people about it. If your master is a DASH tape, you also need to state the speed and format (twin or normal), so they can make sure they're playing it on the right machine.

There are no azimuth problems with digital tape, so those 100 Hz and 10 kHz tones you're used to putting on analog tapes aren't necessary. However, it's a good idea to let people know what your reference level is, whether it's –12 dB, –15 dB, or something else. You should also let them know where the loudest point on the tape is (index number, minute, and second), so they can check to make sure there's no clipping. Plus, a few seconds at the beginning of the tape of a 1-kHz sine wave, at whatever you're using for a reference level, will let them know that your equipment is calibrated correctly (and allow them to make adjustments if it's not!)

A Final Word

We hope this book has been helpful, and has made clearer your options when it comes to dealing with digital audio. The field is changing rapidly, but the basic principles and things to watch out for remain the same.

If you would like more detailed technical information about digital recording, here are a few excellent books on the subject:

Ken Pohlmann, *Principles of Digital Audio,* third edition, Sams (division of Prentice Hall Computer Publishing), Carmel, Indiana.

Ken Pohlmann (editor), *Advanced Digital Audio,* Sams (division of Prentice Hall Computer Publishing), Carmel, Indiana.

Francis Rumsey, *Digital Audio Operations,* Focal Press (division of Butterworth-Heinemann), London, England and Woburn, Massachusetts

John Watkinson, *The Art of Digital Audio,* Focal Press (division of Butterworth-Heinemann), London, England and Woburn, Massachusetts

Two good sources of information about synchronization are:

Time Code Handbook, Cipher Digital Inc., Frederick, Maryland.

John Ratcliff, *Time Code: A User's Guide,* second edition, Focal Press (division of Butterworth-Heinemann), London, England and Woburn, Massachusetts

About the author

Paul D. Lehrman has been writing about audio, music, and computers since 1977, in magazines such as *Studio Sound, Recording Engineer/Producer, Keyboard, NewMedia, Electronic Musician, EQ, Millimeter, Sound On Sound, MacUser,* and the *Boston Phoenix.* He writes the "Insider Audio" column for *Mix* magazine.

He is co-author of MIDI For The Professional (Amsco), and a contributor to several other books including Making Music With Your Computer (EM Books/Hal Leonard). He has written user manuals for Roland, TASCAM, JBL, AKG, Kurzweil, and Passport Designs.

He is also a composer, specializing in music for video and multimedia. He is on the faculty of the College of Fine Arts at the University of Massachusetts Lowell, and serves as associate director of the Center for Recording Arts, Technology & Industry.

Graphics:	LARRY NAVON
Technical Consultants:	ROGER MAYCOCK, PAUL M. YOUNG, JIM LUCAS
Thanks to:	TASCAM, OPCODE SYSTEMS, DIGIDESIGN, MACROMEDIA